"THE LOST CITY OF ATLANTIS"

BY:

T. BLOSSOM

Table of Content

Chapter 1: The Legend of Atlantis

In the beginning of time, the world was vastly different from what it is today. Great civilizations rose and fell, and many wonders were lost to the sands of time. But there was one city that stood out among them all - a city that was said to be the most magnificent and powerful of them all. This was the city of Atlantis.

Atlantis was said to be an advanced civilization, with technology and knowledge far beyond anything that existed at the time. It was also said to be a peaceful society, where the people lived in harmony with each other and with nature. The city was ruled by a wise and just king named Atlas, who was said to possess great wisdom and knowledge.

The legend of Atlantis has been passed down through the ages, and it is said that the city was located somewhere in the middle of the Atlantic Ocean, surrounded by the most beautiful beaches and crystal-clear waters. It is said that the city was surrounded by a great wall that was impenetrable, and that it was guarded by the most skilled warriors in the world.

The people of Atlantis were said to be a peaceful and contented people, who were blessed with abundance and prosperity. They had access to the most advanced technology and knowledge, and they used it to make their lives comfortable and luxurious. They were skilled in the arts and sciences, and they were known throughout the world for their great wisdom and knowledge.

One day, the people of Atlantis discovered a great power that was said to be even greater than their own. This power was said to be a powerful crystal that possessed the ability to harness the energy of the sun and the stars. The people of Atlantis became obsessed with this crystal, and they began to use it to power their machines and their technology.

As time passed, the people of Atlantis became more and more dependent on this crystal, and they began to use it to do everything. They used it to power their machines, to light their homes, and to grow their food. They became so dependent on this crystal that they began to neglect the natural resources around them, and they began to abuse the environment.

As the people of Atlantis became more and more dependent on the crystal, they began to lose touch with the natural world around them. They began to neglect their crops and their livestock, and they began to pollute the oceans and the rivers. The animals began to die off, and the plants began to wither away.

The king of Atlantis, Atlas, tried to warn his people about the dangers of their dependence on the crystal, but they refused to listen. They were too obsessed with their technology and their luxuries, and they believed that nothing could harm them.

But then, one day, disaster struck. The crystal that powered Atlantis began to malfunction, and it emitted a powerful energy pulse that destroyed the city. The great walls of Atlantis crumbled, and the city sank beneath the waves of the ocean.

The people of Atlantis were never seen again, and it is said that they were swallowed up by the ocean, never to be heard from again. But the legend of Atlantis lives on, and it serves as a warning to those who would become too dependent on technology and neglect the natural world around them.

The legend of Atlantis has inspired many stories and myths throughout history, and it continues to capture the imagination of people today. It serves as a reminder of the dangers of greed and the importance of balance and harmony with nature. May we never forget the lessons of Atlantis, and may we always strive to live in harmony with the natural world around us.

Chapter 2: The Search Begins

The morning sun shone brightly over the Mediterranean Sea as the research vessel, The Poseidon, made its way towards the coordinates where the ancient city of Atlantis was believed to have been located. Dr. Alexandra Reed, the lead archaeologist, stood at the bow of the ship, scanning the horizon with a pair of binoculars, hoping to catch a glimpse of any sign of the fabled city.

Beside her, Dr. James Michaels, the marine biologist, was busy setting up his equipment. "Do you really think we'll find anything down there?" he asked, looking up at Alexandra.

"I hope so," she replied, adjusting her hat to shield her eyes from the sun. "According to my research, this is the most likely spot for the city's location. We just have to keep our eyes peeled and be ready for anything."

The Poseidon was equipped with the latest underwater scanning technology, including sonar, magnetometers, and submersibles. They would use these tools to scan the ocean floor and hopefully locate any structures that could be the remains of the lost city.

As they approached the coordinates, the crew of The Poseidon grew increasingly excited. The possibility of discovering the lost city of Atlantis was a dream come true for many of them.

"Captain, we've reached the target location," one of the crew members called out.

"Excellent," the captain replied, his eyes glued to the navigation equipment. "Begin the sonar scans and let's see what we can find."

For hours, they scanned the ocean floor, carefully mapping out every inch of the area. As the sun began to set, they still had not found any signs of the lost city.

"It's getting dark," James said, looking up from his equipment. "Should we call it a day?"

Alexandra hesitated for a moment before nodding in agreement. "We need to regroup and come up with a new plan," she said, turning to the captain. "We'll continue our search tomorrow."

The crew spent the night on board the ship, discussing their findings and brainstorming new ideas for the search. Alexandra poured over her notes, trying to find any clue that could lead them to the lost city.

The next morning, they set out again, determined to find Atlantis. They widened their search area, covering a larger section of the ocean floor. Suddenly, the sonar beeped loudly, indicating a large object was below them.

"Captain, we've got something!" the crew member called out.

The team gathered around the sonar screen, watching as a faint outline of a structure began to emerge. Excitement filled the air as they realized they had found something.

"Send down the submersible," Alexandra said, her heart racing with anticipation. "We need to get a closer look."

James piloted the submersible down to the ocean floor, his hands gripping the controls tightly. As they approached the structure, it became clearer that it was indeed man-made.

"Oh my God," Alexandra gasped, peering through the submersible's window. "It's a building!"

The team spent hours exploring the structure, taking photographs and measurements, and carefully examining every detail. They found evidence of advanced engineering and architectural techniques that were far ahead of their time.

"This is it," Alexandra said, her voice filled with awe. "This is the lost city of Atlantis."

The discovery sent shockwaves through the scientific community, and news of the find spread around the world. Alexandra and her team became overnight celebrities, hailed as the greatest archaeologists of their time.

For months, they continued to explore the ruins of Atlantis, uncovering more and more evidence of the city's greatness. They found a library filled with ancient texts, artwork that depicted mythical creatures and gods, and a central temple that seemed to have been the heart of the city's religious and political life.

As they continued their research, they began to piece together the story of Atlantis. According to ancient texts, Atlantis was a highly advanced civilization that was destroyed in a single day and night of cataclysmic events, sinking beneath the sea and disappearing from history.

It was still unclear what had caused the city's destruction, but the team found evidence of a massive earthquake and tsunami that may have played a role in the city's downfall.

As the team delved deeper into the ruins, they also found evidence of a highly advanced culture that was far ahead of its time. They discovered advanced technology and scientific knowledge that was thought to have been developed much later in human history.

The discovery of Atlantis opened up new avenues of research and inquiry, and many scientists and historians began to reevaluate their understanding of ancient history and the origins of human civilization.

Alexandra and her team continued to explore the ruins for several years, documenting and cataloging their findings. They also began to collaborate with other scientists and researchers from around the world to share their discoveries and further their understanding of Atlantis.

In the end, the discovery of Atlantis proved to be one of the greatest archaeological finds in human history, changing our understanding of ancient civilizations and pushing the boundaries of scientific inquiry.

And for Alexandra, it was the culmination of a lifelong dream, the realization of a quest that had taken her to the very depths of the ocean and beyond. It was a moment she would never forget, the day she discovered the lost city of Atlantis.

After days of sailing, the explorers finally arrived at the coordinates that they believed to be the location of the lost city of Atlantis. As they anchored their ship, they could feel their excitement growing. They had been dreaming of this moment for years, and now they were finally here.

The first thing they did was to start exploring the area around the ship. They searched the nearby beaches and cliffs for any signs of civilization. They found nothing but rocks, seaweed, and sand. The more they looked, the more disheartened they became. They had been hoping for something more concrete, some sign that they were on the right track.

Just when they were about to give up, one of the explorers, a young woman named Lily, noticed something strange about the rocks near the shoreline. They appeared to be carved in a pattern that was not natural. She called over the other explorers to take a closer look.

As they examined the rocks, they began to see that the carving was, in fact, a message. It was written in a language that they did not recognize, but they could tell that it was ancient. They took pictures of the carving and decided to try to decode it later.

As they continued to explore the area, they found more and more clues that pointed to the existence of Atlantis. They found fragments of pottery that appeared to be from a culture that they had never seen before. They found pieces of metal that were unlike anything they had ever seen. They also found more carvings that appeared to be messages.

The explorers decided to set up a base camp and spend some time studying the area. They wanted to learn as much as they could before moving on. They started to piece together the clues that they had found.

They found that the language of the carvings was similar to ancient Greek, but it was not exactly the same. They also found that the metal that they had found was a type of alloy that was not known to exist in ancient times. They concluded that they were dealing with a civilization that was far more advanced than any that they had known.

The more they learned, the more they became convinced that they were on the right track. They started to believe that they were close to finding the lost city of Atlantis. They decided to focus their efforts on decoding the carvings.

After weeks of study, they were finally able to translate the messages that they had found. They were amazed by what they discovered. The carvings told the story of a civilization that was far more advanced than any that they had known. It was a civilization that had harnessed the power of the sun, the wind, and the sea. It was a civilization that had built great cities and had traveled to the stars.

The explorers were filled with a sense of wonder and awe. They knew that they were on the brink of discovering something truly amazing. They decided to continue their search, convinced that they were close to finding the lost city of Atlantis.

As they set out to explore the area further, they found more clues that pointed to the existence of Atlantis. They found underwater structures that appeared to be man-made. They found ruins of buildings that were unlike anything they had ever seen. They also found artifacts that were clearly of Atlantean origin.

The more they found, the more convinced they became that they were on the right track. They decided to explore the underwater structures to see if they could find any more clues.

As they descended into the depths, they saw a city unlike any they had ever seen. It was a city of incredible beauty and sophistication. It was a city that had been lost to the world for thousands of years. The explorers were overwhelmed with emotion. They knew that they had discovered something truly amazing. They had found the lost city.

Chapter 4: The Expedition of Atlantis

After months of preparation and planning, the expedition to discover the lost city of Atlantis was finally underway. Led by renowned archeologist Dr. Sophia Patel, the team consisted of divers, engineers, and historians from all over the world. Their mission was to locate the legendary city that was believed to have been lost beneath the waves thousands of years ago.

The team boarded the research vessel, Atlantis Explorer, which was equipped with the latest underwater technology and set sail towards the Atlantic Ocean. The journey was long and arduous, but the team remained focused on their goal.

Once they reached their destination, the team began their search. They used a combination of sonar, underwater cameras, and robotic vehicles to explore the ocean floor. It was a slow and painstaking process, but the team remained determined.

Days turned into weeks, and the team was starting to lose hope. Just when they were about to give up, they discovered something that would change the course of their expedition. They found a series of underwater tunnels that led deep into the ocean floor. Dr. Patel was convinced that these tunnels were connected to the lost city of Atlantis.

The team spent the next few days exploring the tunnels. They encountered various obstacles, such as strong currents and narrow passages, but they persevered. Finally, they reached a massive underwater chamber that was unlike anything they had ever seen before.

The chamber was filled with ancient ruins and artifacts that were perfectly preserved by the sea. It was clear that they had finally discovered the lost city of Atlantis. The team was ecstatic, and Dr. Patel could hardly contain her excitement.

They spent the next few weeks exploring the city and cataloging their findings. They discovered that Atlantis was a highly advanced civilization that had developed technologies far ahead of its time. They found evidence of renewable energy sources, advanced transportation systems, and even evidence of flight.

However, the team's joy was short-lived. They soon discovered that the city was in danger. The underwater tunnels that they had used to access the city were beginning to collapse, and the team knew that they had to act quickly to save the city.

They worked tirelessly to stabilize the tunnels and protect the city from further damage. It was a race against time, but the team was determined to save Atlantis.

After weeks of hard work, the team finally succeeded in stabilizing the tunnels and saving the city. They had not only discovered the lost city of Atlantis, but they had also saved it from destruction.

The team returned to the surface with a newfound appreciation for the mysteries of the ocean and the achievements of ancient civilizations. They had accomplished what many believed to be impossible, and their expedition would go down in history as one of the greatest archeological discoveries of all time.

Chapter 5: Discovering Atlantis

As news of the discovery of Atlantis spread, the world was abuzz with excitement. People from all over the globe flocked to see the ancient ruins that had been hidden beneath the waves for millennia. Dr. Sophia Patel and her team became overnight celebrities, hailed as heroes for their groundbreaking discovery.

The team spent months cataloging their findings, analyzing artifacts, and piecing together the history of Atlantis. They discovered that the city was a highly advanced civilization that had flourished more than 10,000 years ago. Atlantis was home to a highly educated and skilled population, who had made incredible strides in the fields of engineering, agriculture, and medicine.

Their research also revealed that the people of Atlantis had been highly spiritual and had worshiped a pantheon of gods and goddesses. The team discovered several temples and shrines dedicated to these deities, and they found evidence of elaborate ceremonies and rituals that had been conducted to honor them.

One of the most exciting discoveries made by the team was the existence of a powerful energy source that had been used by the people of Atlantis. They found remnants of massive power generators that had been used to harness the energy of the ocean's tides. This technology was far ahead of its time, and it was clear that the people of Atlantis had possessed a deep understanding of the natural world.

As the team delved deeper into the history of Atlantis, they discovered that the city had not been destroyed by a natural disaster, as many had previously believed. Instead, it was revealed that the downfall of Atlantis had been brought about by a combination of factors.

The people of Atlantis had become complacent, believing that their advanced technology and knowledge made them invincible. They had become arrogant and selfish, and their society had become corrupt. This had led to widespread inequality, and many citizens had become disillusioned with their leaders.

As the situation worsened, the people of Atlantis began to lose touch with their spiritual beliefs, and they became more materialistic. This led to the development of a powerful military-industrial complex, which consumed vast amounts of resources and led to the exploitation of other societies.

Eventually, the people of Atlantis became embroiled in a series of devastating wars that tore the city apart. The city was destroyed, and the survivors were forced to flee in ships and scatter across the world.

The team's discoveries shed new light on the history of human civilization and prompted new questions about the nature of progress and the dangers of unchecked ambition. Their findings also challenged many long-held beliefs about the nature of ancient societies and the capabilities of early civilizations.

As the team wrapped up their work on the site, they made plans to preserve the ruins of Atlantis for future generations. They recognized the importance of protecting this incredible discovery and ensuring that it remained a source of inspiration and wonder for people for years to come.

In the end, the discovery of Atlantis had profound implications for the world, inspiring new ideas and pushing the boundaries of human knowledge. Dr. Patel and her team had achieved what many had thought impossible, and their expedition would go down in history as one of the greatest archeological discoveries of all time.

Chapter 6: Unraveling the Mystery of Atlantis

As the world continued to be captivated by the discovery of Atlantis, Dr. Sophia Patel and her team remained hard at work, determined to unravel the mystery of this ancient civilization. They pored over every artifact and document they could find, trying to piece together a complete picture of what life was like in Atlantis.

One of the greatest mysteries that they had yet to unravel was the true extent of Atlantis' power and influence. While they had discovered evidence of a highly advanced civilization, it was still unclear how far the reach of Atlantis had extended. Some scholars had theorized that Atlantis had been a global superpower, while others believed that it had been a smaller, regional power.

To help solve this mystery, the team turned to the sea, where they hoped to find evidence of Atlantis' influence beyond its shores. They enlisted the help of marine archaeologists and began exploring the surrounding waters.

It wasn't long before they made their first major discovery. They uncovered the remains of several underwater structures that appeared to have been part of a massive network of canals and aqueducts. These structures suggested that Atlantis had possessed an extensive system of water management, which would have been essential for supporting a large population.

As they continued to explore, the team uncovered evidence of ancient trade routes that had connected Atlantis to other regions around the world. They found artifacts from distant lands, suggesting that Atlantis had been a major player in international trade. They also found evidence of diplomatic missions and embassies, suggesting that Atlantis had maintained close relations with other nations.

However, the team's most significant discovery came when they stumbled upon a series of ancient tablets that had been inscribed with an unknown script. After months of painstaking work, they were finally able to decipher the script and reveal the story of Atlantis' rise and fall.

According to the tablets, Atlantis had indeed been a global superpower, with colonies and allies stretching across the world. The people of Atlantis had been highly advanced, possessing knowledge and technology that far surpassed anything that existed in their time. However, as the team had previously discovered, their society had become corrupt and exploitative, leading to its eventual downfall.

The tablets also revealed that there had been survivors of the destruction of Atlantis, who had fled across the world and established new civilizations. The team was stunned by this revelation, realizing that the legacy of Atlantis had lived on long after its destruction.

As the team wrapped up their work on the site, they realized that the discovery of Atlantis had far-reaching implications for the world. It showed that human civilization had been far more advanced and interconnected than previously thought, and it demonstrated the importance of preserving the knowledge and culture of ancient societies.

The team made plans to publish their findings and share their discoveries with the world, hoping to inspire a new generation of scholars and adventurers to continue exploring the mysteries of the past. They also made plans to continue their work, hoping to uncover even more secrets about the lost civilization of Atlantis.

In the end, the mystery of Atlantis had been largely unraveled, revealing a fascinating and complex civilization that had existed thousands of years ago. While many questions still remained, the discovery of Atlantis had opened up new avenues of inquiry and provided a glimpse into the remarkable achievements of our ancient ancestors.

The discovery of Atlantis had not only shed light on the past, but it also had the potential to impact the present and future. The knowledge and technology that the Atlanteans possessed could potentially revolutionize modern-day society, but it also served as a cautionary tale about the dangers of corruption and overexploitation.

Furthermore, the discovery of Atlantis had sparked a renewed interest in archaeology and exploration, as people around the world became inspired by the possibilities of uncovering new mysteries and discovering new knowledge.

As news of the discovery spread, governments and organizations began investing in new archaeological expeditions, hoping to uncover other lost civilizations and unlock new knowledge about our past. Scholars and scientists from around the world collaborated on research and shared resources, furthering the understanding of our ancient ancestors.

However, there were also concerns about how the discovery of Atlantis would be handled. Some worried that it would be exploited for commercial gain, with companies trying to capitalize on the public fascination with the lost city. Others worried that it would be used as a political tool, with nations trying to claim ownership or influence over the site.

To prevent these issues, the team of researchers who discovered Atlantis made efforts to ensure that the site was properly protected and preserved. They worked with governments and organizations to establish guidelines for exploration and research, with a focus on minimizing damage and preserving the site for future generations.

Overall, the discovery of Atlantis was a groundbreaking moment in the history of archaeology and exploration. It not only expanded our understanding of the past but also inspired new generations of scholars and adventurers to continue exploring the mysteries of our world.

Chapter 7: The Legacy of Atlantis

The discovery of Atlantis had a profound impact on the world, sparking a renewed interest in archaeology and exploration, and inspiring people around the globe to explore the mysteries of the past. However, the legacy of Atlantis went far beyond its impact on academic fields.

The knowledge and technology that the Atlanta's possessed had the potential to revolutionize modern society, from medicine and agriculture to architecture and engineering. Researchers from around the world poured over the artifacts and documents discovered in Atlantis, trying to understand the technology and knowledge that the Atlanta's had possessed.

One of the most exciting discoveries was a series of tablets that contained information about advanced agricultural techniques. The Atlanta's had developed innovative methods for crop cultivation, irrigation, and soil management, which could have a significant impact on modern-day farming practices.

The tablets also revealed information about medicine and healing practices, suggesting that the Atlanta's had a sophisticated understanding of the human body and how to treat illnesses. This knowledge could help modern-day researchers develop new treatments and cures for diseases.

In addition to technological advancements, the legacy of

Atlantis also had an impact on art and culture. The team of researchers who discovered Atlantis uncovered a wealth of art and literature, revealing a vibrant and diverse culture that had existed thousands of years ago.

The art of Atlantis was characterized by intricate designs, vibrant colors, and a sense of harmony between nature and humanity. The literature of Atlantis was equally impressive, with works of poetry, philosophy, and history that were still relevant and inspiring to modern-day readers.

Moreover, the legacy of Atlantis served as a reminder of the importance of preserving the knowledge and culture of ancient civilizations. The destruction of Atlantis had led to the loss of a great deal of knowledge and technology, highlighting the need to protect and preserve the knowledge of other ancient societies.

As news of the discovery spread, governments and organizations around the world began investing in the preservation of other ancient sites and artifacts, ensuring that the knowledge and culture of our ancient ancestors would be protected for future generations.

The legacy of Atlantis also had an impact on international relations, as nations worked together to protect and preserve the site. The team of researchers who discovered Atlantis worked with governments and organizations from around the world to establish guidelines for exploration and research, with a focus on minimizing damage and preserving the site for future generations.

In the end, the legacy of Atlantis was a testament to the remarkable achievements of our ancient ancestors. It showed that human civilization had been far more advanced and interconnected than previously thought, and it demonstrated the importance of preserving the knowledge and culture of ancient societies.

As the team of researchers wrapped up their work on the site, they reflected on the impact that the discovery of Atlantis had had on the world. They were proud to have contributed to the understanding of our past and inspired a new generation of scholars and adventurers to continue exploring the mysteries of our world.

The legacy of Atlantis would continue to inspire and shape the world for years to come, reminding us of the incredible potential of human achievement and the importance of protecting and preserving the knowledge and culture of our ancient ancestors.

In addition to the impact on technology, art, culture, and international relations, the legacy of Atlantis also had a spiritual impact. The discovery of a lost civilization with advanced knowledge and technology sparked new debates and discussions about the origins of human civilization and the purpose of human existence.

The existence of a civilization as advanced as Atlantis challenged traditional beliefs and theories about human history, forcing people to question what they thought they knew. Some saw the discovery of Atlantis as evidence of a more divine or mystical origin of human civilization, while others saw it as proof of extraterrestrial influence or intervention.

These debates and discussions led to new avenues of exploration and research, as people sought to understand the deeper spiritual and metaphysical implications of the discovery of Atlantis.

Moreover, the legacy of Atlantis also had an impact on the way that people viewed the environment and the natural world. The destruction of Atlantis had been caused in part by the overexploitation of natural resources, a warning of the dangers of unchecked greed and exploitation.

As a result, many people began to view the natural world with a newfound respect and reverence, understanding the importance of preserving and protecting it for future generations. The legacy of Atlantis served as a reminder of the delicate balance between human civilization and the environment, and the need to find sustainable and responsible ways to coexist.

In the end, the legacy of Atlantis was multifaceted and far-reaching, impacting virtually every aspect of human society. It inspired new discoveries and debates, challenged traditional beliefs and theories, and sparked a renewed appreciation for the natural world and the achievements of our ancient ancestors.

As the world continued to change and evolve, the legacy of Atlantis would continue to inspire and shape the way that people thought about the past, present, and future. It was a testament to the power of human curiosity, exploration, and discovery, and a reminder of the incredible potential that we all possess to make a positive impact on the world around us.

Chapter: 8 Theories on the Collapse of Atlantis

Despite the extensive research and excavation conducted on the site of Atlantis, the exact cause of its collapse remains a mystery. However, over the years, researchers have developed several theories to explain the downfall of the great civilization.

One of the most prominent theories is the idea that the destruction of Atlantis was caused by a natural disaster, such as a volcanic eruption or earthquake. The location of Atlantis, situated in the middle of the Atlantic Ocean, puts it in a geologically active area. This theory suggests that a catastrophic natural event caused the city to sink beneath the waves.

Another popular theory is that the downfall of Atlantis was caused by a war or conflict with another civilization. This theory is supported by the accounts of the ancient Greek philosopher Plato, who described Atlantis as a powerful and militaristic society that had conquered many other civilizations. Some researchers believe that this militarism eventually led to a conflict that resulted in the destruction of the city.

A third theory is that the collapse of Atlantis was caused by a societal or environmental collapse. This theory suggests that the Atlantis may have overexploited their natural resources, leading to environmental degradation and societal collapse. This idea is supported by the fact that many ancient civilizations, such as the

Mayans and Easter Islanders, collapsed due to environmental or societal pressures.

A fourth theory is that the Atlantis was destroyed by an extraterrestrial event, such as a meteor or comet impact. This theory is based on the idea that the Atlanta's possessed advanced knowledge of astronomy and may have been aware of an incoming extraterrestrial object. Some researchers suggest that this event caused widespread destruction and may have led to the downfall of the Atlantis civilization.

A fifth theory is that Atlantis was destroyed by a combination of factors, including natural disasters, environmental degradation, and societal collapse. This theory suggests that the downfall of Atlantis was a complex and multifaceted event, influenced by a range of factors that ultimately led to the collapse of the civilization.

Despite the numerous theories that have been proposed, the exact cause of the collapse of Atlantis remains unknown. The limited evidence available and the fact that the city is submerged underwater make it difficult to conclusively determine what happened.

However, the ongoing research and exploration of the site of Atlantis continues to yield new information and insights into the civilization. As researchers continue to uncover new artifacts and documents, it is possible that the mystery of the downfall of Atlantis may one day be solved.

In the meantime, the mystery of Atlantis continues to capture the imagination of people around the world. The legend of the lost city remains a symbol of human curiosity, exploration, and discovery, inspiring new generations to pursue their own quests for knowledge and understanding of the world around them.

In recent years, advances in technology and scientific exploration have shed new light on the theories surrounding the collapse of Atlantis. For example, sonar imaging and satellite mapping have allowed researchers to better understand the geological and environmental conditions that may have contributed to the destruction of the city.

Additionally, advances in archaeology and DNA analysis have led to new discoveries and insights into the social and cultural practices of the Atlanta's. For example, researchers have uncovered evidence of extensive trade networks and sophisticated agricultural practices, shedding new light on the economic and environmental sustainability of the civilization.

As new theories and discoveries continue to emerge, the mystery of Atlantis will likely continue to capture the attention and imagination of people around the world. The legend of the lost city serves as a reminder of the incredible achievements and capabilities of our ancient ancestors, as well as the fragility of human civilization and the natural world.

Moreover, the continued exploration and investigation of the site of Atlantis provides a unique opportunity for researchers to study the past and gain new insights into the complex relationships between societies and their environments. As we continue to unravel the mysteries of the past, we can gain a better understanding of the challenges and opportunities that lie ahead for our own society.

Ultimately, the theories on the collapse of Atlantis remind us of the importance of questioning assumptions, exploring new frontiers, and striving for a deeper understanding of the world around us. Whether or not we ever fully unravel the mystery of Atlantis, the legacy of the lost city will continue to inspire and

challenge us for generations to come.

Chapter: 9 The Technology and Achievements of   Atlantis

Chapter 9 of Plato's "Caritas" introduces Atlantis, an advanced civilization that supposedly existed around 9,000 years before the time of Plato. According to the story, Atlantis was a prosperous and powerful civilization that possessed advanced technology and achieved great feats in various fields. In this essay, we will explore some of the technological achievements of Atlantis, as described in the text.

One of the most remarkable achievements of Atlantis was its ability to harness the power of nature. According to the text, the Atlanteans were able to use the energy of the sun, wind, and water to power their civilization.

They had advanced systems for collecting and storing solar energy, including large mirrors that focused the sun's rays onto a central point to create heat. They also had sophisticated wind turbines that could generate electricity from the strong winds that blew across their island.

In addition to renewable energy, Atlantis was also known for its advanced knowledge of metallurgy. The text describes how the Atlanteans were able to mine and refine a variety of metals, including gold, silver, and copper. They had developed techniques for casting these metals into intricate shapes and had even discovered a way to create a metal that was stronger than any other known material. This metal, called orichalcum, was said to be a glowing red color and was highly prized by the Atlanteans for its beauty and durability.

Another area in which Atlantis excelled was agriculture. The text describes how the Atlanteans were able to cultivate a wide variety of crops, including fruits, vegetables, and grains. They had developed advanced irrigation systems that allowed them to grow crops in areas that would otherwise be unsuitable for farming. They also had sophisticated techniques for preserving food, including drying and salting, which allowed them to store large quantities of food for long periods of time.

Atlantis was also a center of learning and knowledge. The text describes how the Atlanteans had developed a system of education that was focused on developing the intellectual and physical abilities of its citizens.

They had schools and universities where students could study a wide range of subjects, including philosophy, mathematics, and science. The Atlanteans were particularly interested in astronomy and had developed advanced telescopes that allowed them to observe the stars and planets in great detail.

One of the most impressive achievements of Atlantis was its architecture. The text describes how the Atlanteans had built magnificent structures using advanced techniques and materials. They had developed a type of cement that was stronger and more durable than any other known material, and they used it to build massive structures, including temples, palaces, and public buildings. They also had advanced engineering techniques that allowed them to build bridges and aqueducts that spanned great distances.

Finally, the text describes how Atlantis was a seafaring civilization that had developed advanced navigation techniques. They had developed large ships that were capable of traveling great distances and had a sophisticated understanding of ocean currents and wind patterns. They had also developed a system of underwater tunnels and canals that allowed them to travel between different parts of their island quickly and efficiently.

In conclusion, according to the text of Plato's "Critias," Atlantis was an advanced civilization that achieved great technological feats in various fields. They were able to harness the power of nature, had advanced knowledge of metallurgy, excelled in agriculture and architecture, and were a center of learning and knowledge. While the existence of Atlantis is still a matter of debate among historians and scholars, the story of this advanced civilization has captured the imaginations of people for centuries, and the legacy of Atlantis continues to inspire and fascinate us to this day.

It's worth noting that the technology and achievements of Atlantis, as described in Plato's "Critias," are not just impressive but also reflect a highly advanced and sophisticated society. The story portrays Atlantis as a utopian society that was highly advanced, prosperous, and influential. However, its downfall was brought about by its own hubris and arrogance, which led to its destruction in a catastrophic event.

In terms of their technology, the Atlanteans were not just focused on practical applications but also had an appreciation for beauty and aesthetics. This is evident in the description of the orichalcum metal, which was not only incredibly strong but also had a glowing red color that was highly prized for its beauty. Similarly, their architecture was not just functional but also grand and awe-inspiring, with magnificent structures that were built to last.

It's also interesting to note that the story of Atlantis has been linked to real-world archaeological discoveries and theories. Some scholars have suggested that the Atlantis story may have been based on the Minoan civilization that existed on the island of Crete around

4,000 years ago. The Minoans were known for their advanced technology and sophisticated culture, and some have speculated that they may have inspired the Atlantis myth.

Overall, the story of Atlantis and its technological achievements continue to capture the imagination of people around the world. Whether or not Atlantis actually existed, its legacy serves as a reminder of the potential for human progress and the dangers of hubris and arrogance.

Chapter: 10 Atlantis in Popular Culture

Plato's "Critias" may have been the first written mention of the legendary lost city of Atlantis, but it certainly wasn't the last. Over the centuries, Atlantis has captured the imaginations of writers, filmmakers, and artists, inspiring countless works of popular culture. From science fiction novels to Hollywood blockbusters, Atlantis has become a staple of popular culture, with each iteration reflecting the cultural and social contexts in which they were created. In this essay, we will explore the many ways in which Atlantis has been portrayed in popular culture.

One of the earliest works of fiction to feature Atlantis was

"New Atlantis," a 17th-century utopian novel by Sir Francis Bacon. In this book, Bacon describes a fictional island called Bensalem that is home to a highly advanced society with technologies far beyond what was available in Europe at the time. Although Bacon's Bensalem was not explicitly identified as Atlantis, it is widely considered to be an early inspiration for the Atlantis myth and helped popularize the idea of a lost utopian civilization.

In the late 19th century, theosophist and writer Helena Blavatsky also popularized the idea of Atlantis in her book "The Secret Doctrine." Blavatsky claimed that Atlantis was a real place that existed long before recorded history and was destroyed in a great cataclysm. Her writings helped to fuel the popular imagination about Atlantis and sparked interest in the idea of ancient civilizations with advanced technologies.

In the 20th century, Atlantis became a popular subject in science fiction literature. In H.G. Wells' "The War of the Worlds," the Martians are said to have destroyed Atlantis as they traveled across the solar system. Jules Verne's "20,000 Leagues Under the Sea" features a lost city that is believed to be Atlantis, and the novel "The Land That Time Forgot" by Edgar Rice Burroughs features a subterranean world that is said to be the remnants of Atlantis.

Atlantis has also been a popular subject in Hollywood movies, with one of the most famous being Disney's animated film "Atlantis: The Lost Empire" released in 2001. In the movie, a group of explorers discovers the ruins of Atlantis and learns about its advanced technology and culture. The film was praised for its stunning animation and creative world-building, and helped to introduce the Atlantis myth to a new generation of viewers.

In addition to movies, Atlantis has also been a popular subject in video games, with many games featuring lost cities and ancient civilizations. One example is the popular game "Assassin's Creed: Odyssey," which takes place in ancient Greece and features a quest that involves uncovering the secrets of Atlantis. The game's creators took inspiration from Plato's description of Atlantis and created a visually stunning underwater city that is unlike anything else in the game.

Atlantis has also been a popular subject in comic books, with DC Comics' Aquaman featuring the lost city as a major part of its mythology. In the comics, Atlantis is depicted as a powerful underwater kingdom with advanced technology and a long history of conflict with the surface world. The character of Aquaman, who is the king of Atlantis, has become one of the most popular and recognizable superheroes in the DC universe.

Finally, Atlantis has also been a popular subject in music, with many songs referencing the lost city. One example is Donovan's "Atlantis," a 1968 song that tells the story of the city's destruction in a great flood. The song became a hit and helped to cement Atlantis as a popular cultural reference.

In conclusion, Atlantis has become an enduring and versatile subject in popular culture, inspiring countless works of fiction, film, video games, comic books, and music. While the details of the Atlantis myth may vary depending on the medium

One thing that remains consistent is the fascination with the idea of a lost utopian civilization with advanced technology and culture. The continued popularity of Atlantis reflects our enduring interest in the mysteries of the past and our fascination with the possibilities of human achievement.

Moreover, the portrayal of Atlantis in popular culture has evolved over time, reflecting changing cultural and social contexts. Early portrayals of Atlantis were often idealistic and utopian, reflecting the optimism and faith in progress of the Enlightenment era. Later portrayals of Atlantis, particularly in science fiction, often had a darker tone, reflecting the anxieties and fears of the Cold War era and the potential dangers of unchecked technological progress.

Today, Atlantis continues to capture the imagination of creators and audiences alike, with new works of popular culture featuring the lost city being produced every year. Whether as a utopian ideal, a cautionary tale, or simply a source of inspiration for storytelling, Atlantis remains an enduring and fascinating subject in popular culture.

Despite the lack of concrete evidence for the existence of Atlantis, the myth of the lost city has persisted for centuries, inspiring countless works of literature, film, and art. However, along with this fascination has come a slew of myths and pseudoscientific theories surrounding Atlantis. In Chapter 11, we will examine some of these myths and pseudoscientific claims and discuss why they are not supported by evidence.

Myth #1: Atlantis was an Advanced Civilization with Advanced Technology

One of the most persistent myths surrounding Atlantis is the belief that it was an advanced civilization with highly advanced technology. This idea is largely based on Plato's description of the city as possessing "wonderful works of engineering," but there is little evidence to support this claim. While ancient civilizations like the Greeks and the Romans made significant advancements in engineering, there is no evidence to suggest that they possessed technologies that were significantly more advanced than what was available in other civilizations at the time.

Myth #2: Atlantis was Destroyed by a Cataclysmic Event

Another common myth about Atlantis is the idea that it was destroyed by a catastrophic event, such as a volcanic eruption or a massive earthquake. This myth is often used to explain why there is no physical evidence of Atlantis, as it suggests that the city was completely destroyed and submerged beneath the ocean. However, there is no evidence to support this claim, and it is far more likely that if Atlantis did exist, it was simply abandoned or destroyed by more mundane means.

Myth #3: The Bermuda Triangle is Connected to Atlantis

The Bermuda Triangle, an area of the Atlantic Ocean where several ships and airplanes have mysteriously disappeared, has often been linked to Atlantis. According to this theory, the supposed advanced technology of Atlantis created a powerful energy field that still exists in the area, causing planes and ships to disappear. However, there is no evidence to support this theory, and the idea has been thoroughly debunked by scientists.

Myth #4: Ancient Astronauts or Aliens Built Atlantis

Another popular myth surrounding Atlantis is the idea that the city was built by ancient astronauts or aliens. This theory suggests that the advanced technology and engineering of Atlantis were beyond the capabilities of humans at the time, and must have been created by extraterrestrial beings. However, there is no evidence to support this theory, and it relies on the assumption that ancient civilizations were not capable of making significant advancements in technology and engineering.

Pseudoscience #1: Psychics and Mediums Can Communicate with Atlantis

Some psychics and mediums claim to be able to communicate with the spirits of the inhabitants of Atlantis, using their supposed abilities to provide insight into the lost city. However, there is no scientific evidence to support the existence of psychic abilities, and the idea that psychics can communicate with the spirits of the dead is not supported by any reputable scientific organization.

Another pseudoscientific claim about Atlantis is the idea that it was the cradle of civilization, and that all human civilization can be traced back to Atlantis. This theory is often used to support the idea of a global conspiracy to hide the truth about Atlantis, but there is no evidence to support the claim that Atlantis was the birthplace of civilization. In fact, the development of human civilization can be traced back to a variety of different locations and time periods, and there is no reason to believe that Atlantis played a central role in this process.

In conclusion, the myth of Atlantis has inspired countless

works of literature, film, and art, but it has also given rise to a number of myths and pseudoscientific claims. These claims are not supported by evidence, and are often used to promote conspiracy theories or to sell books and products. It is important to

approach the topic of Atlantis with a critical eye, and to rely on reputable sources and scientific evidence when evaluating claims about the lost city.

It is also worth noting that the fascination with Atlantis can be seen as part of a broader cultural phenomenon, in which we are drawn to stories of lost or hidden civilizations that hold the promise of unlocking secrets about the past or offering insights into the present. While there is nothing inherently wrong with this fascination, it is important to approach these stories with a healthy skepticism and a willingness to examine them critically.

Ultimately, the myths and pseudoscientific claims surrounding Atlantis serve as a reminder of the power of storytelling and the enduring appeal of mysteries and legends. However, it is important to separate fact from fiction, and to approach claims about Atlantis with a critical eye and a willingness to seek out evidence and evaluate it objectively.

Chapter: 12 Future Researches and Exploration of Atlantis

Despite centuries of speculation and exploration, the question of whether or not Atlantis existed remains unanswered. However, advances in technology and exploration techniques mean that the possibility of discovering new evidence about the lost city is greater than ever before. we will explore some of the future research and exploration that could shed new light on the mystery of Atlantis.

Underwater Exploration

One of the most promising areas of future research and exploration is underwater exploration. While there have been several attempts to locate the remains of Atlantis beneath the ocean, modern technology has greatly improved our ability to survey the ocean floor and to search for evidence of ancient civilizations. Advances in sonar and remote sensing technologies mean that we can now explore areas of the ocean that were previously inaccessible, and we can map the ocean floor with unprecedented detail. By focusing on areas that are believed to be the most likely locations of Atlantis, such as the Mediterranean or the Atlantic Ocean, underwater exploration may yet uncover new evidence about the lost city.

Geological Studies

Another area of research that could shed new light on Atlantis is geological studies. According to some theories, Atlantis was destroyed by a catastrophic event, such as a volcanic eruption or a massive earthquake. By studying the geological history of the areas believed to be the location of Atlantis, scientists may be able to identify evidence of such an event. For example, volcanic ash or other signs of geological disturbance could indicate that a catastrophic event occurred in the area, which could support the theory that Atlantis was destroyed by such an event.

Archaeological Excavation

While underwater exploration is a promising area of research, it is also possible that evidence of Atlantis may be found on land. Archaeological excavation in areas believed to be the location of Atlantis could uncover artifacts or other evidence of an ancient civilization. For example, if Atlantis was located in the Mediterranean, archaeologists could explore the islands of the

Aegean Sea, where ancient civilizations such as the Minoans and Mycenaeans once thrived. By carefully excavating these sites, archaeologists may be able to uncover evidence of a lost civilization that could shed new light on the mystery of Atlantis.

Digital Mapping and Modeling

Advances in digital mapping and modeling technologies mean that we can now recreate entire cities in virtual space, providing a new avenue for research into Atlantis. By using archaeological evidence, historical records, and computer modeling techniques, researchers may be able to create a virtual model of the lost city. This model could be used to explore various theories about the layout and design of Atlantis, as well as to test different scenarios about how the city may have been destroyed or abandoned.

Interdisciplinary Research

Finally, a multidisciplinary approach to research may be the key to unlocking the mystery of Atlantis. By bringing together experts from fields such as archaeology, geology, anthropology, and history, researchers may be able to explore the mystery of Atlantis from multiple angles. By working together, these experts may be able to identify new lines of research or to draw on expertise from different fields to shed new light on the mystery of Atlantis.

In conclusion, while the question of whether or not Atlantis existed remains unanswered, advances in technology and exploration mean that the possibility of discovering new evidence is greater than ever before. By focusing on areas such as underwater exploration, geological studies, archaeological excavation, digital mapping and modeling, and interdisciplinary research, researchers may be able to uncover new insights into the mystery of Atlantis. While the search for Atlantis may never be truly resolved, it remains an intriguing mystery that continues to captivate our imaginations and inspire new avenues of research and exploration.